Don't Die
with
Vacation Time
on the Books

Andrea Goeglein, PhD

Copyright © 2011
Published in the United States by
Andrea Goeglein, Ph.D.
1000 Pine Island Court
Las Vegas, NV 89134

ISBN-978-1-60013-616-0
10 9 8 7 6 5 4 3 2 1

All rights reserved. No part of this book may be reproduced in any form or by any means without prior written permission from the publisher except for brief quotations embodied in critical essay, article, or review. These articles and/or reviews must state the correct title and contributing authors of this book by name.

Economic statistics referenced in the text are derived from:
Bureau of Labor Statistics
U.S. Department of Labor
www.bls.gov

Dow Jones Industrial 5-yr Chart
Dow Jones Indexes
A CME Company
Princeton NJ 08543-0300

US Housing Start Table
U.S. Census Bureau and
Department of Housing and Urban Delopment
www.census.gov

To my friend, Marel Giolito

Table of Contents

Introduction	1
Prologue	3
Change Your Awareness and Your Perspective Changes	5
You Teach What You Need to Learn	17
Experience Is What You Get When You Don't Get What You Want	29
The Business of Broken Promises	31
Power * Purpose * Prosperity	33
You Can Make Excuses or You Can Achieve Your Goals, But You Can't Do Both	39
Shoulda, Woulda, Coulda	81
Epilogue	89
Transforming Your Excuses Into Goals	91
About the Author	100
Quotes	101

Introduction

"Remember to remember."
Michael Bernard Beckwith

Welcome. This book is my attempt to dispel a myth that has been perpetrated on the unsuspecting masses for many generations. The myth I refer to is the one that assures if you do your homework, earn good grades, and graduate from the right schools, you will land a job or create a business that will provide you riches, happiness, health, and love; you will achieve your "happily ever after."

My life experience and observations go more like this: You do all the things you are told to do, and many you are not supposed to do—sometimes it works out and sometimes it doesn't. All that really matters is that you appreciate what does work, try new things when something does not work, and always take responsibility for creating your own reality, one which allows you to view each life experience as another cobblestone on the crooked road of achieving life happiness and well being.

Most books come from the author's experience, and this book is no exception. Be it a book of facts, fiction, or fable, somewhere, somehow the author's experience sculpts the underlying story. Given that reality, let me share with you some facts, as I see them.

First, this is my story, whether I am writing about something that occurred in my life, espousing some theory in psychology, or describing the experiences of another. In the end, all the stories in this book are just a part of my story.

Second, your life is a story, too. I challenge you to read this book with the intention of writing the story of your journey—up until now—on your crooked road of success.

Don't Die with Vacation Time on the Books is the first of The Crooked Road of Success™ small book, big impact series. It is a book, it is a story, and it is a journal for you to create your story.

Happy Reading. Happy Writing.

Prologue
November 2007

For the second time in two years, I stood on the stage of a hotel I owned with my husband, about to address a group of businesswomen, ready to teach them about life and the need to be open to change. Attendance was double that of our first conference. I felt secure and accomplished. Positive anticipation was palpable in the humming sound of conversations and the lively beat of the music in the background.

During my presentation, I delivered the message that time was of the essence, and the essence of time is change. I recounted my "Don't die with vacation time on the books" story to make the point.

Everyone in the audience laughed. Everyone promised not to die with vacation time on the books.

Walking off stage, I glanced at my cell phone and experienced a moment of synchronicity. While I had been speaking, I missed a call from the friend who had implored me, six months earlier, to make that very promise to her.

"We don't see things as they are, we see them as we are."

– Anais Nin

Change Your Awareness and Your Perspective Changes

Perspective literally means the way in which objects appear to the eye.

In real life, our perspective is how we choose to "see" and interpret the events of our lives.

Moment by moment, millions of these events are incubating in the background of our busy days; most go unnoticed, yet every moment has the potential to change us.

"One sees great things from the valley, only small things from the peak."

–G. K. Chesterton

Every moment holds the potential to cause us to see differently.

Only when we pay attention and notice these small moments, do we make the connections that lead to a change in our perspective. Such awareness reveals the significance in the single, seemingly isolated moments of our lives.

Sometimes, in one of those moments an event occurs that stops your heart and demands you pay attention. What follows that event is a shift in your life, and in your perspective, you never anticipated.

Every moment holds the potential to become such a perspective-changing event.

Such a moment happened to me, and I wasn't paying attention.

That moment was a simple phone call, which I received from my longtime friend, Marel, who also owned a business.

She began the call with an odd request, "Andrea, we need to make each other a promise. Let's promise we won't die with vacation time on the books."

I laughed, and I promised.

"A vacation is what you take when you can no longer take what you have been taking."

—Earl Wilson

A vacation is nothing more than a time of respite, an intermission.

If you listen closely, people are always offering their perspectives on vacations. They say, "I can't afford to take a vacation," or "I am too busy to take a vacation," or "I deserve a vacation."

Your perspective of "vacation" dictates whether you take a vacation, defer a vacation, or even value a vacation.

Vacation time is something we all accrue, but only the wisest of us recognize its importance.

"Somebody should tell us, right at the start of our lives, that we are dying. Then we might live life to the limit, every minute of every day. Do it! I say. Whatever you want to do, do it now! There are only so many tomorrows."

—Michael Landon

For a business owner, "vacation time on the books" means that an employee has accrued time off from work, and that time becomes an obligation to be paid.

Truth is, as small business owners, we might find it inconvenient to pay an employee for taking time away from the job. The smaller the business, the bigger the inconvenience; the smaller the business, the harder it might be to find the cash to make the payment, and still run your business.

"A promise made is a debt unpaid."

–Robert Service

Yet, we never want to make a payment to an estate because the employee died before he (or she) had an opportunity to use that vacation time. Making such a payment can feel a little like going to the funeral of a longtime friend, carrying with you the money that you owed him. On paper, the debt is cleared, but you always remember that it was a check written with the blood of your heart.

My friend had to write that check twice in one year, for two longtime employees; she wanted to make sure we learned from their mistakes.

"We are all teachers; the question is not whether we will teach, but what."

—Anonymous

You Teach What You Need to Learn

The thing about perspective-changing events is that they usually don't announce themselves as such, and often the change that occurs happens over time.

The hope is that there will be enough time to grasp the lesson hidden in the change. It is the passage of time that allows promises, and laughter, to transform into learning.

As you learn, you begin to share.

Each time you share, you are actually teaching.

Each time you teach, you learn something else you needed to know.

That is why, when you teach, you learn twice.

"Learning without thought is labor lost; thought without learning is perilous."

—Confucius

Six months after I had laughed and made a promise to my friend, I had my first opportunity to teach and learn twice.

I stood on the stage before a group of businesswomen, teaching them about life and the need to be open to change. I used my "Don't die with vacation time on the books" story to make the point.

Everyone laughed. Everyone made the promise not to die with vacation time on the books.

Walking offstage, I glanced at my cell phone and smiled. I experienced a moment of synchronicity. I had received a call from the friend who had implored me to make that very promise.

"There are no mistakes, no coincidences. All events are blessings given to us to learn from."

—Elisabeth Kübler-Ross

Synchronicity is the experience of two or more events that are causally unrelated occurring together in a meaningful manner.

Notice "occurring together in a meaningful manner" does not specify if the meaning is good or if the meaning is bad. That is where your perspective comes into play.

Perspective-changing events can have many parts. One part can be a tense, laughter-filled promise. Another part can have no laughter at all.

That was my first lesson.

The call from Marel came at the end of a triumphant day. I remembered thinking she probably wanted to congratulate me, and hear an account of the day's events. I could not immediately listen to her message.

I was busy—the hours were closing on the second annual women's conference I had created; I was basking in the appreciation of those who had attended, shaking hands, reading the "What Worked About Today?" and "What Could Make It Better for You Next Year?" feedback flipcharts that had been set up in the cocktail reception area. A spontaneous smile came to my face as I read the comment, "The only thing that could make it better is to make it longer!" followed by "Ditto."

"You must look within for value, but must look beyond for perspective."

—Denis Waitley

At the end of the day, all that was left to do was sit, share dinner with my team, and let them know how proud and honored I was to have them with me. I settled into my seat; placing my cell phone on the table, I remembered the missed call from my friend. With little thought, and even less emotion, I dialed my voice mail and listened to her message, "Hi Andrea. It's Marel. I am okay. Call me when you can."

The words did not fit the feeling of distress I sensed in her voice. I placed my phone down. I was busy. I told myself I would call her first thing in the morning.

———————

"Time puts things in proper perspective."

—Cameron Crowe

The next morning, I learned that time waits for no busy woman.

My "don't die with vacation time on the books" buddy was calling to tell me she was given a terminal diagnosis.

She still had vacation time on the books and she wanted to use it.

Her employees had taught her.

She had taught me.

We thought we had learned.

We now knew we needed to learn twice.

"Experience is not what happens to a man. It is what a man does with what happens to him."

–Aldous Huxley

Experience Is What You Get When You Don't Get What You Want

No one wants to die with vacation time on the books.

No one wants to receive a terminal diagnosis.

No one knows what she will do with a perspective-changing experience until it happens.

And when it happens, the only thing you are usually clear about is that it's an experience you did not want to have happen.

Marel did not want the experience of that diagnosis.

I did not want the experience of receiving that call.

No one wanted to experience what happened next.

"Life is what happens when you are busy making other plans."

–John Lennon

The Business of Broken Promises

In June 2007, while *I was busy laughing and making promises...*
Unemployment was 4.5%
The Dow Jones Industrial Average was 13,408
Total Housing Starts were 350,000

In November 2007, *while I was busy thinking I was teaching...*
Unemployment was 4.8%
The Dow Jones Industrial Average was 13,371
Total Housing Starts were 272,000

In January 2008, *while I was busy making plans for a new year...*
Unemployment was 4.9%
The Dow Jones Industrial Average was 13,043
Total Housing Starts were 231,000

———————

You get sick and you start a plan to recover your health.

Your business slows and you make plans to get it moving.

The world spirals into an economic crisis and you have no choice but to let life inform you what your next plan will be.

Power * Purpose * Prosperity

November 2008

One year after receiving my friend's ominous call, I stood on the same stage of my hotel, before many of the same businesswomen who had attended my conference in previous years, all of whom were waiting to hear my wisdom, again.

I launched the conference in 2006 with the theme, Power * Purpose * Prosperity. In 2007, I added an exponent: Power * Purpose * Prosperity^2. I planned to promote the 2008 event as Power * Purpose * Prosperity^3.

The state of the economy, however, had posed a problem to this nomenclature. By early September 2008, the theme that I had created with perpetuity in mind began to feel like false advertising. As the day of the event drew nearer, I needed to revise my plan.

The new plan was: "We will lead by example."

The "we" in this instance included me and my husband, who also happened to be my business partner. "The plan" was that we would implore the audience:

We must be optimistic;

We must reframe our perspective;

We must adjust our plans to succeed in light of the changes that have occurred.

To illustrate the message, my husband opened the conference with his personal story of remaining optimistic in the face of adversity:

"You cannot give up hope," he urged. "I haven't, and I was born in 1934 in the middle of the Great Depression, and I have been fired at the onset of every major recession this country, and the world, has faced in my lifetime: 1973, 1987, *and* 2001."

He elicited a laugh when he added, "I do feel a little safer this time. Now, I work for my wife."

———

Two weeks later our business died.
We were all fired.
We all needed a new plan.
Everyone had vacation time on the books.
This was not the kind of vacation any of us had wanted to plan.

Experience is what you get when you don't get what you want.

To get what you want, you better learn from the experience.

Life is what happens when you are busy making other plans. And those plans better be flexible.

"The absent are never without fault, nor the present without excuse."

—Benjamin Franklin

You Can Make Excuses or You Can Achieve Your Goals, But You Can't Do Both

Abundant evidence exists to prove that we are continually creating excuses to explain why we do not reach our goals. Evidence shows:

we make excuses at the personal level;

we make excuses at the community level;

we make excuses at the national level;

we make excuses at the global level.

There is just a lot of evidence that we make excuses for not achieving our goals.

At the business level, we give these excuses disguises, such as "missing the street estimate," "shortfalls," or "chapter reorganization."

I dare you to top this excuse for why our business failed: God did it.

You read correctly—my excuse for not achieving our goal of business success could have been, "God created the failure."

More precisely, that is the sentiment one former employee expressed—*after we fired him*.

My business partner and I had thought that our major point of disagreement with this employee was how we measured performance: our employee measured his performance by the amount of activity he imitated; we measured his performance by the results of all that activity.

This employee's parting letter to us, infused with his religious beliefs, offered quite a different perspective. He wrote that God had informed him that we would make the decision to fire him. Our former employee believes that there is God's way (which we apparently violated by firing him), and there is man's way, which ends in death (in our case, the death of our business).

There you have it.

God did it.

According to this perspective, I fired an underperforming employee and God punished me. My former employee inadvertently provided me with the perfect excuse for my business failure.

You would think that I would have felt relieved; I supposedly had a reason why everything went awry—God did it.

I did not have to blame myself, I did not have to shame myself, and most of all, I did not have to take responsibility.

I did not have just any excuse. I had an excuse that could not be proven or disproven.

Yet, a few interesting things happened on the way to having the perfect excuse:

I felt totally defeated.

I felt helpless.

I felt hopeless.

It seemed I now had a choice to make.

I could use the ultimate, unprovable excuse that God did it, or I could achieve my goals of life happiness and well being, but I could not do both.

"Everything we hear is an opinion, not a fact. Everything we see is a perspective, not the truth."

-Marcus Aurelius

It came down to which perspective I chose to acknowledge: the perspective that an external force caused my downfall and I had no control; or, the perspective that, regardless of external forces, I could make excuses, or I could achieve my goal, but I could not do both.

At the time, my perspective was that there was an external shift that internally caused me to feel like crap.

It was November 2008; the external shift taking place included major upheavals on the economic and political landscapes:

Unemployment was 7.2%

The Dow Jones Industrial Average was 8,829

Total Housing Starts were 153,000

The United States was about to inaugurate a new President, one whose historic campaign and election promised hope as much as it promised a lot of change.

There was that promise thing again. This time, however, so few people were laughing.

We all were about to learn twice what hope and change are really about.

Hope is a transitive verb. That means it needs a noun to express a complete action—you need to hope *for* something; hope explains the anticipation you experience when you are expecting to gain something. Hope also means to expect with confidence; to trust.

Change, too, is a transitive verb. To change is to alter, transform, make radically different, and give a different position, course, or direction *to* something.

Change is not the promise that there will be no challenges, but the hope that with each challenge you learn to grow with greater trust.

What I can promise is that all of this hope, change, and trust takes time.

———

I knew this external shift, which was shifting my perspective, was an important moment. My ability to trust was at stake.

As a businessperson, I was forced to re-evaluate three longstanding business beliefs:

1. The higher your customer service rating, the higher your success.

Between 2007 and 2008, our business increased its already high customer service standing. We made it into the top 5% of all performers within our franchise system.

2. Year-over-Year performance is an indicator of how your business is doing.

October 2008 our business had its best same-month sales ever.

3. The higher your SEO (search engine optimization), or ranking and visibility on the Internet, the better your business results.

Our business was rated number 1 or 2 on all the top Internet sites to attract business for our industry.

Suddenly, there was a new reality, one in which I could no longer bank on these standards. I had to reframe my belief system, and develop new goals.

And, I knew I wasn't alone.

It wasn't only my trust that had been shattered. The foundation of our economic system had shattered. Who in the business community could still believe the promises upon which our economic system had been built?

My first goal was to stop making excuses and to shift my perspective, whether it felt like crap or not.

That goal seems to be the same whenever change creates a loss: Stop making excuses and shift your perspective.

This applies whether you have lost a business, or whether you have lost your health.

One difference between losing your health and losing your business may be that when you lose your health, you quickly run out of time to make excuses.

How, or why, your health is in the state that it is in has no real bearing on what you may need to do next. What does need to happen is a shift in perspective from looking for excuses to building hope and trust. No one can be promised her health will be restored, or never fail again.

You still need the confidence to hope you will find the right people to trust.

Answer this question (you only get one choice):

If you were to experience a major loss, would you want to lose your business, or would you want to lose your health?

Business.

Health.

Business.

Health.

My friend was not given that choice, and I know that.

If I had been asked before Marel's life-changing phone call, I know I would have answered "business."

I now had to find a way to trust that answer.

My friend now had to find a way to trust she could find an answer.

———

"The blame is his who chooses; God is blameless."

–Plato

I could have accepted what my former employee claimed: God did it. I was familiar with the superstitious concept of a God who handed out rewards and punishments in between starting wars and choosing the winners.

Then, I remembered four simple words, "In God We Trust." Those words had guided my business career; I trusted that God was not a malicious entity—an entire nation trusted that God would guide her in all her endeavors.

But, could I lay the blame at God's door *and* trust in God to make it right?

Somewhere between "but" and "and" lay all the excuses.

I had a choice, yet again.

The choice was a familiar one: stop making excuses and shift my perspective.

There was no "but" or "and."

From where I stood, "In God We Trust" was about the only shift left to make.

Another moment of synchronicity struck me—those words were printed on our currency because someone had once written a letter, too!

"America is not just a power, it is a promise. It is not enough for our country to be extraordinary in might; it must be exemplary in meaning."

—Nelson Rockefeller

In the early days of the Civil War, the Reverend M. R. Watkins appealed to the Secretary of the Treasury to include a reference to God on U.S. currency so that we would always remember what guided our country's greatness, regardless of external circumstances.

"In God We Trust" has been printed on our currency since 1864, because of that letter.

Today, many believe money was the root of our latest national and global crisis. Some think if our monetary system were still based on the gold standard, the economic crisis would not have happened.

What I have learned is that no amount of gold in storage would have forestalled the inflated U.S. housing market collapse, fraudulent mortgage applications, unbounded credit issuance, the banking industry's global irresponsibility and greed, and a major war deficit. Make all the excuses you want, but there is no gold in those goals.

However, "In God We Trust" seems to cover our need to trust in the unknown and unseen. The concept of God, although debated heavily, really cannot be proved. We can never prove "enough" God to ensure we are able to traverse all the pitfalls, potholes, and roadblocks in the crooked road of success. That is where the "trust" part comes in.

When I enter into a transaction, I must trust that my business associate will deliver as he promised, and he must trust that I will give him something of value that can be passed along to keep the trust cycle going.

There is never a conversation about what is backing our money; there is never a conversation about whether or not I can trust the other person to do as he promised.

"Let us not seek to fix the blame for the past. Let us accept our own responsibility for the future."

–John F. Kennedy

No amount of money, or trust in God, promises you will recover from a business crisis or a health crisis.

Yet, trust is the promise that backs all economies.

Trust is the promise that backs all human development.

Trust is both a promise and a goal.

Business.

Health.

Business.

Health.

There should be no excuses.

In June 2010, while I was busy planning how to teach what I had learned about adapting to shifting perspectives:

Unemployment was 9.6%

The Dow Jones Industrial Average was 9,774

Total Housing Starts were 171,000

Thirty-six months have passed since I made the promise to Marel, and I am more aware that numbers do not tell stories—people do.

I am more aware that the stories we tell are completely based on our own perspectives.

I am more aware my perspective of external events can overshadow the internal shifts that are occurring.

It is the greater awareness of these realities that allows me to accept a re-awakening to the promise that every "I" event only needs to be experienced from the perspective of "In God We Trust."

And I am again awakened to Michael Bernard Beckwith's quote, *"Remember to remember."*

I will remember that change is not the promise that there will be no challenges, but the hope that with each challenge, I learn to grow with greater trust.

I will remember that all of this hope, change, and trust takes time.

"The here and now is all we have, and if we play it right, it's all we'll need."

—Ann Richards

Shoulda, Woulda, Coulda

The best way to not die with vacation time on the books is to stop worrying about what you shoulda done.

Stop worrying about what you woulda done.

Stop worrying about what you coulda done.

Actually, the best way to make sure you don't die with vacation time on the books is to:

Stop worrying.

Start living with greater awareness.

And, when you plan a vacation, actually take it.

In the end, we will teach what we need to learn, and...

if experience is what you get when you don't get what you want, and…

life is what happens when you are busy making other plans, and...

you can trust that whether or not you believe in a God, you promise not to worry about it...

then, there is no excuse for dying with vacation time on the books.

"True success comes when you hit a crisis or rough spot, and people don't revert to their old behaviors."

–Lynn Mercer

Epilogue

My friend, Marel, experienced a successful bone marrow transplant; she is not only alive, she is taking lots of vacations.

My husband and I cashed in the 1,000,000 reward points accrued on our personal credit card (used to buy supplies for our dead business) to take the ultimate vacation to Barcelona.

The accrued vacation time owed to my former employees was paid.

Trust was restored.

A perspective-changing shift has occurred.

I am paying closer attention.

"Not managing your time and making excuses are two bad habits. Don't put them both together by claiming you don't have the time."

—Bo Bennett

Transforming Your Excuses Into Goals

Now, it's time for you to stop making excuses and achieve your goals. On the pages provided, think through your perspective-changing events and write your story using the following statements as a guide:

If I lived my life in a way that guaranteed I did not die with vacation time on the books how would I be living?

What are some of the perspective-changing events in my life?

___

___

___

___

___

___

___

___

___

___

___

What did these events teach me and how have I used those lessons?

If experience is what I got when I did not get what I wanted, what do I want?

What plans have I made that did not turn out as intended?

What excuses did I make for the outcome I got?

Can I be trusted to do as I promise?

Whom do I trust?

About the Author

Founder. President. Developer. Mentor. These words identify Andrea T. Goeglein, Ph.D., however, the greatest testimonials to her achievements are the long-standing successes of the events, institutions, and businesses she has cultivated with her clients.

Dr. Goeglein's unique combination of experiences, skills, and accomplishments stands out in the world of business. A former hotel owner, and founder of a range of successful business enterprises, she has been a counselor and personal mentor to the CEOs of privately held companies. She has capitalized on her talents as a dynamic national speaker, major event organizer, community activist, author, and business consultant to build an international portfolio.

She earned her doctorate degree in organizational psychology after achieving significant success in her business endeavors. Now, she is devoted to bringing the tenets of positive psychology to life for her clients and audiences.

A much sought after media personality, Dr. Goeglein frequently appears as an expert guest on KAZ-TV's *AM Arizona*; she has also appeared on *The Rachel Ray Show*, and on major radio networks across the nation. Her interviews, writings, and sightings can be viewed at:

www.YouTube.com/user/ServingSuccess
www.servingsuccess.blogspot.com
www.facebook.com/DrSuccessPhD

Quotes

"Remember to remember."
–Michael Bernard Beckwith

"We don't see things as they are, we see them as we are."
– Anais Nin

"One sees great things from the valley, only small things from the peak."
–G. K. Chesterton

"A vacation is what you take when you can no longer take what you have been taking."
–Earl Wilson

"Somebody should tell us, right at the start of our lives, that we are dying. Then we might live life to the limit, every minute of every day. Do it! I say. Whatever you want to do, do it now! There are only so many tomorrows."
–Michael Landon

"A promise made is a debt unpaid."
–Robert Service

"We are all teachers; the question is not whether we will teach, but what."

—Anonymous

"Learning without thought is labor lost; thought without learning is perilous."

—Confucius

"There are no mistakes, no coincidences. All events are blessings given to us to learn from."

—Elisabeth Kübler-Ross

"Time puts things in proper perspective."

—Cameron Crowe

"Experience is not what happens to a man. It is what a man does with what happens to him."

—Aldous Huxley

"Life is what happens when you are busy making other plans."

—John Lennon

"The absent are never without fault, nor the present without excuse."

—Benjamin Franklin

"Everything we hear is an opinion, not a fact. Everything we see is a perspective, not the truth."
—Marcus Aurelius

"You must look within for value, but must look beyond for perspective."
—Denis Waitley

"The blame is his who chooses; God is blameless."
—Plato

"America is not just a power, it is a promise. It is not enough for our country to be extraordinary in might; it must be exemplary in meaning."
—Nelson Rockefeller

"Let us not seek to fix the blame for the past. Let us accept our own responsibility for the future."
—John F. Kennedy

"The here and now is all we have, and if we play it right its all we'll need."
—Ann Richards

"True success comes when you hit a crisis or rough spot, and people don't revert to their old behaviors."
—Lynn Mercer

"Not managing your time and making excuses are two bad habits. Don't put them both together by claiming you don't have the time."

–Bo Bennett

This book was dedicated to my friendship with Marel Giolito.

My life is dedicated to honoring my love of:

>My Mother, Christina Terzano
>
>My Father, Andrew Terzano
>
>My Husband, Richard Goeglein
>
>My daughter, Dana Courtney

I trust my God has brought you all into my life to teach me unending love.